ESSAYS IN INTERNATIONAL FINANCE

No. 19, June 1954

AGRICULTURAL PRICE POLICY AND INTERNATIONAL TRADE

D. GALE JOHNSON

INTERNATIONAL FINANCE SECTION

DEPARTMENT OF ECONOMICS AND SOCIAL INSTITUTIONS

PRINCETON UNIVERSITY

Princeton, New Jersey

This essay was prepared as the nineteenth in the
series ESSAYS IN INTERNATIONAL FINANCE published
by the International Finance Section of the Department of Economics and Social Institutions in Princeton University.

The author, D. Gale Johnson, is Professor of Economics at the University of Chicago.

The Section sponsors the essays in this series but
it takes no further responsibility for the opinions
expressed in them. The writers are free to develop
their topics as they will and their ideas may or may
not be shared by the editorial committee of the Section or the members of the Department.

The Section welcomes the submission of manu-
scripts for this series and will assume responsibility
for a careful reading of them and for returning to
the authors those found unacceptable for publication.

GARDNER PATTERSON, Director
International Finance Section

ESSAYS IN INTERNATIONAL FINANCE

No. 19, June 1954

AGRICULTURAL PRICE POLICY AND INTERNATIONAL TRADE

D. GALE JOHNSON

INTERNATIONAL FINANCE SECTION
DEPARTMENT OF ECONOMICS AND SOCIAL INSTITUTIONS
PRINCETON UNIVERSITY
Princeton, New Jersey

AGRICULTURAL PRICE POLICY AND INTERNATIONAL TRADE

D. GALE JOHNSON
University of Chicago

A N appraisal of the interrelations and inconsistencies between international trade policy and agricultural price policy in the United States appropriately may begin with a description and analysis of the farm price programs. Such a beginning is justified because the major steps to eliminate some of the inconsistencies between farm price and international trade programs must start with the farm price programs. This position does not rest upon the presumption that nothing can be done through international economic measures to heal the breach between trade and agricultural policies. Instead, two other premises are uppermost. First, the present farm price policies are basically inimical to the long run interests of American farm people, as well as to the general level of productivity in the United States. Second, the price and other policies that can be designed to meet the most important economic objectives of American farm people would not require a significant interference with the expansion of international trade as a means of gaining the advantages of international specialization.

But before examining agricultural price policy and international trade policy, it is pertinent to consider the linkage that exists between domestic and international markets for agricultural products. If the United States were neither an important exporter nor importer of agricultural products, its actions in the farm price field would have little significance to international trade policies.

I. UNITED STATES TRADE IN AGRICULTURAL PRODUCTS

The United States is in the rather unique position of being a major exporter of both manufactured and agricultural products and a major importer of agricultural products and raw materials. As a result, our farm programs as well as our trade policies can and do have a significant influence on the total world movement and prices of agricultural products.

Although there are great variations in the year-to-year value and quantity of our agricultural imports and exports, United States trade in many farm goods is an important part of the world trade in such products. As an importer, the United States in recent years has been taking about one-fifth of the world's exports in sugar and from 15 to 30 per cent of the wool—the two major products for which we are an important producer and importer. As an exporter, this country plays an even greater role, having accounted during the period 1949-1952 for the following percentages of total world exports: wheat, 33-50 per cent; cotton, 30-45 per cent; tobacco, 35-40 per cent; rice, 10-13 per cent; lard, 75-90 per cent; tallow, 60-80 per cent; and all fats and oils, 17-19 per cent.

There are several different ways of depicting the importance to the United States farmer of his export markets and of the changes in their importance over time; perhaps the most significant for present purposes is the ratio of the value of exports to cash farm income. As Table 1 shows, this ratio in recent years has been well below that of the twenties, but exports still account for about 10 per cent of the farmer's total cash receipts.

Table 1

United States Agricultural Exports and
Total Cash Farm Income, 1910-1953[a]

Period	Exports as Percentage of Cash Farm Receipts
1910-1914	17.5
1925-1929	17.3
1930-1934	12.9
1935-1939	9.4
1946	12.9
1947	13.1
1948	11.5
1949	12.8
1950	10.0
1951	12.2
1952	10.5
1953	9.1

[a] Sources: United States Department of Agriculture, *United States Farm Products in Foreign Trade*, Statistical Bulletin No. 112, Washington, D.C., 1953, p. 11. The data for 1951, 1952, and 1953 were taken from current press releases of the Department of Agriculture.

These overall statistics hide the even greater dependence of several farm commodities upon foreign markets. During 1949-1951, more than a third of all our wheat, cotton, and rice were exported; and approximately one quarter of our soybeans, tobacco, rye, grain sorghums, lard, tallow, field peas, and hops were sent abroad. Looked at in still another way, in recent years the value of agricultural exports has accounted for some 25 to 30 per cent of the total of United States commodity exports.

Imports of products of agricultural origin have bulked even larger in our total trade, constituting about 40 to 50 per cent of our total commodity imports. However, about half of these agricultural imports are not competitive with domestic agriculture, including as they do such commodities as coffee, crude rubber, copra, bananas, tea, spices, and wool for carpets.

Sketchy as these few data are, there can be no doubt that the United States has in the past and does at present play a significant role in international trade in agricultural products and that important linkages exist between the international and the domestic market for such goods.

II. A SHORT HISTORY OF FARM PRICE
PROGRAMS, 1933-1953

Although the Federal Farm Board was engaged in certain price supporting operations as early as September, 1929, the beginning of the present farm price programs was in 1933 when the Agricultural Adjustment Act was passed and the Commodity Credit Corporation was created. The Corporation immediately offered non-recourse loans to producers of cotton and corn and they have been available every year since that time. The first cotton loan was at ten cents a pound, although the market price had just previously been around six cents. The first corn loan rate was set at 45 cents a bushel, only moderately above the market price at the time the loan was announced. The first wheat loans were not made until 1938—the small crops of 1933, 1934, 1935 and 1936 having resulted in relatively favorable wheat prices—but they too have since been continuously available. Tobacco producers have also enjoyed a price support loan program since the mid-thirties. In addition, many other commodities, such as rye, oats, barley, wool, flaxseed, dried milk, butter, soybeans, cheese, honey, and mohair, have had their prices supported through the use of non-recourse loans or direct government purchases.

The non-recourse feature of these loans means simply that the Commodity Credit Corporation cannot collect the amount of money borrowed by a farmer, unless the farmer wishes to repay. The farmer in

3

obtaining such a loan has two alternatives: (1) He may deliver the farm product which served as a security for the loan, or (2) he may pay the amount borrowed. Thus, if the market price exceeds the loan value the farmer will redeem the farm product used as a security for the loan by paying the Corporation the amount borrowed. However, if the market price is below the loan value, he will deliver the product to the Corporation. The non-recourse loan is only one, albeit the most important, of a number of methods used to influence the level of market prices. Efforts have been made to restrict supply through acreage allotments, marketing quotas, grade and quality regulation, and actual destruction of output. In addition, steps have been taken to increase demand through distribution of farm products at low cost, or free, to individuals on relief and to certain types of institutions such as schools and homes for the aged and the indigent. During the late thirties and early forties, the food stamp plan was tried as a means of expanding demand through a two price plan available to certain segments of the population, primarily persons on relief.

But efforts to control supply or to expand demand are relatively blunt instruments. The output of farm products is not entirely within the control of man—with no apparent change in acreage planted or seeded, the amount of fertilizer applied, or the production practices followed, output of an individual crop may vary by 20 to 50 per cent from one year to another. This is why direct methods of price influence have become an important and significant part of the farm program. The non-recourse loan and government storage programs represent direct means of assuring a given price, if sufficient storage space is available. Though other methods of direct price maintenance have been used, such as purchase operations, the loan and storage operations have been the mainstay of the farm price support program.

Formally, the objective of these programs is price parity. But the definition of parity and the extent of attainment of that objective has not remained unchanged over the past two decades. The concept of parity originally expressed in the Agricultural Adjustment Act of 1933 was a very simple notion (even though there is either one too many or one too few commas): ". . . prices to farmers at a level that will give agricultural commodities a purchasing power with respect to articles that farmers buy, equivalent to the purchasing power of agricultural commodities in the base period." The base period for all agricultural commodities except tobacco was August 1909-July 1914; that for tobacco was the ten years starting with August 1919.

In 1935 the sentence structure was straightened out, and, in addition, certain adjustments in the definition of parity were introduced. Prior to 1935 purchasing power of the prices farmers received was defined

4

solely in terms of prices paid by farmers for products used in production or consumed by the household. In 1935 "interest payments per acre on farm indebtedness secured by real estate and tax payments per acre on farm real estate" were added. That year the index of prices paid was 125; the addition of the other two factors increased the overall index to 130. Thus the change in definition increased parity prices by four per cent. However, by 1942 the rise in prices paid so outstripped the change in mortgage interest and taxes that the inclusion of the latter reduced parity prices. In fact, in 1948 the prices paid index was 264 while the combined index used in calculating parity prices was only 250.

The next major changes in the calculation of parity prices came in 1948 and 1949, when, for the first time, farm wage rates were included in the calculation of parity prices. The inclusion of wage rates would have resulted in a very significant increase in parity prices (about 6 per cent in 1948) but a concurrent revision of the whole index reduced the net effect of the change to about 3.5 per cent for 1948. Although there is no question but that the intent of these changes in the calculation of parity prices was to raise the level of parity prices, their net effect (including the statistical revisions) often has been to leave the parity prices unchanged. If the parity prices were calculated on January 15, 1954 by the method used from 1933 to 1935, the prices paid index would be 284; the index now in use for most commodities is 284. The best laid plans of mice and men often go astray.

There was another change in the calculation of parity prices, however, that has had a substantial impact. In the Agricultural Act of 1948 a new method of determining parity prices was enacted. This method was not designed to change the average level of parity prices; its purpose was to modify the *relative* parity prices of the various farm commodities. It was recognized that the previous methods of calculating parity prices of each commodity had resulted in serious distortions of relative farm prices. Not only did the relative prices which prevailed in the 1910-14 period fail to represent current demand and supply relationships, but over the years many other base periods were used as parity prices were calculated for an ever-increasing number of commodities. In fact, in 1949, only about one-third of the farm commodities for which parity prices were calculated were based entirely on the 1910-14 base periods. The remainder involved various base periods for the interwar period. The 1948 revision specified that the relative parity prices were to be based on actual relative market prices for the ten preceding years. Thus farm products whose market prices were lagging behind the general level of farm prices would have their parity prices lowered.

This revision of parity prices was recognized by most agricultural economists as a decided improvement. But from a political viewpoint, the new parity formula had the basic disadvantage of lowering parity prices for a number of "politically important" crops—namely, cotton, wheat, corn, and peanuts. As a result, in 1949 Congress legislated that for the four years beginning January 1, 1950 (when the new parity prices were to be effective), the parity price would be the higher of the old or the new parity for the so-called basic commodities (cotton, wheat, rice, corn, peanuts, and tobacco). This provision was later extended until December 31, 1955. It so happened that the new parity formula increased the parity prices of all important livestock and livestock products, except poultry and eggs; some of the increases were quite substantially, 35 per cent for beef cattle, for example. The parity price for wheat, on the other hand, as of January 15, 1954 would be reduced from $2.48 to $2.13 a bushel by the change in formula. Cotton prices would be reduced by only little more than a cent a pound while corn prices would be reduced by 19 cents a bushel (about 11 per cent). There is no question that the current large stocks of wheat and corn would now be appreciably smaller if the lower parity prices had been in effect since 1950, and even the 1.2 cents reduction in the price of cotton would not have been without some influence.

This short discussion of the development of the parity price calculations is intended primarily to indicate the capriciousness of Congress' approach to the concept. But there is another important facet of parity price as an objective, or as a standard for price support, that warrants notice. This is the question of the relation between the support level and full parity. The original Agricultural Adjustment Act did not specify the level of price support as a percentage of parity. The first loans for corn and cotton were established at approximately 70 per cent of parity. In the Agricultural Adjustment Act of 1938, it was specified that loan rates for corn, wheat, and cotton should range between 52 and 75 per cent of parity, relatively modest objectives on the whole. For the years 1938, 1939 and 1940, corn loan rates were at 70-75 per cent of parity and those for cotton and wheat were at 52-57 per cent. In early 1941 the level of price supports for corn, wheat, cotton, and tobacco was increased to 85 per cent and, later that year, the same level of support was extended to the so-called nonbasic products; the purpose being to encourage increased production. The price support legislation was modified in October, 1942, in two ways. First, the price support levels were increased to 90 per cent of parity, and, second, price supports for all basic commodities, and for nonbasic commodities for which the Secretary of Agriculture had found price supports necessary to achieve increased production, were to be maintained at 90 per cent of parity for two years following the close of the war. Except for the changes in the parity formula described earlier, price supports have generally been

unchanged with respect to parity level since 1942. With respect to certain products, however, the Secretary of Agriculture has had some discretion in setting loan rates, as illustrated by the recent decrease in the price support for butter.

To summarize, during the period from 1933 through 1942 there were two important developments in price support legislation. First, the level of price support, expressed as a percentage of parity, increased substantially. Second, the number of commodities provided price supports increased very rapidly—from less than a half dozen in the mid-thirties to more than 100 during World War II. In recent years price supports have been announced for between 30 and 40 different farm products.

At the present time, it may be noted, there seems to be less willingness to experiment with different methods of price support than was true fifteen years ago. Today major reliance is placed upon purchases and loans, with acreage restrictions being imposed when the former result in stocks that become difficult to manage. But in the thirties it was fairly generally accepted that some income transfers might be made through techniques other than price supports. Two illustrations may be given. During 1935 and 1936 direct price payments were made to producers on each pound of cotton sold as a means of encouraging farmers to sell their cotton rather than to place it under loan. The loan rate was set at 10 cents a pound, but farmers were paid the difference between the actual market price and 12 cents a pound, up to a maximum of 2 cents a pound. The Agricultural Adjustment Act of 1938 included a provision for parity payments which was designed to supplement price supports and to bring the return to the farmer up to 75 per cent of parity. Such payments, totalling $967 million, were made in 1939 through 1942.

A general over-all view of the price support and related activities from 1933 to the present would note the following points. During the last twenty-one years, attempts to regulate production (if one excludes tobacco) were made in only eight years. Most agricultural economists would agree that the methods used to limit output have been relatively ineffective, having been accompanied by positive incentives to increase production. Not only were price supports maintained at relatively profitable levels and direct payments made to producers, but many of the activities associated with the farm programs have been effective means of increasing output by inducing or aiding farmers to adopt improved production techniques.

Contrary to common belief, the *direct* costs of price support operations (up to mid-1953) have been relatively modest—approximately $3.5 billion, which includes such questionable items as $800 million for the School Lunch Program. In part the low financial cost of the farm price support operations has been due to the coincidence of a nationwide drought and two wars. The moderate crop output of the mid-thirties prevented large stocks from accumulating at that time, while the conduct of World War II consumed the large stocks of corn, wheat, and cotton accumulated by 1942. Again, in 1950 the Korean conflict absorbed the large stocks accumulated in 1948 and 1949.

III. THE INCONSISTENT ELEMENTS

The above sketch of farm price support programs does not indicate specifically the elements of inconsistency between those programs and the objective of freer foreign trade. The basic source of conflict is not hard to determine. Many of the support prices are for products for which the United States is either an exporter or an importer. In either case, an effective price support in the American market soon presents serious and obvious problems. If the price support is for a product that is exported and that price support has any influence in increasing domestic prices, exports decline and domestic stocks rise. This loss of foreign markets may be of major importance to some sectors of the farm community and may, indeed, prevent the United States from taking full advantage of its real comparative cost advantages. If the price support is for an imported product, the domestic price support attracts increased imports, as has recently been illustrated by the relatively large imports of oats from Canada, and may create significant strains on our relations with friendly governments if, as has often been the case, measures are taken to prevent such imports.

In the first four or five years of the development of farm programs under the New Deal, the role given to price supports was secondary to other aspects of the programs. It was generally believed that the adjustment features of the programs—restrictions on acreages, transfer of land from one product to another, payments directly to farmers, and creation of orderly markets—were more important than the non-recourse loans. As a result, the first uses of restrictions on imports were not envisioned as an adjunct to price supports, but as a means of retaining to farmers any benefits that might accrue to them from making certain adjustments. The first restriction on imports was made in 1934 in connection with the sugar program, which did not include a price support or commodity loan provision. The first general legislative approval for import restrictions was enacted in 1935 as an amendment to the Agricultural Adjustment Act of 1933. This amendment allowed restrictions (import quotas) only for commodities for which there was an adjustment program under the Act. Section 22, as this authority became generally known, was soon extended to include programs operated under the Soil Conservation Act of 1937 and the Marketing Agreements Act.

Authority was also granted to impose, in addition to import quotas, import fees up to 50 per cent ad valorem and to impose either in connection with any program using Section 32 funds (see below).

Until 1941 import quotas were established under Section 22 only for wheat and cotton. These quotas are still in effect. During the war numerous restrictions were placed on imports, primarily to aid the administration of various schemes for the international allocation of relatively scarce agricultural products. Some imports, such as butter, were prohibited entirely.

At the end of the war spokesmen for certain farming interests argued that the provisions for action under Section 22 authority were too restrictive. Many of the price support operations were not conducted under authority granted in the various acts referred to above. As a result, Section 22 authority was extended to any program undertaken by the Department of Agriculture.

It should be noted that until recently the Executive Branch of the Government has used the authority under Section 22 with considerable restraint. The only new Section 22 action from the end of the war through mid-1953 was the imposition of import fees on almonds; the quotas on wheat and cotton have been continued, however. Under authority given in the Second War Powers Act, the importation of butter, flaxseed, linseed oil, peanuts, peanut oil, and rice and rice products were prohibited. These controls were continued until July 1, 1951, and the following month the Secretary of Agriculture was given broader authority to restrict imports by Section 104, as amended, of the Defense Production Act of 1950. While action under Section 22 is essentially discretionary with the President, the conditions laid down in Section 104 were such as to leave the Secretary of Agriculture little room for discretion. For a specified list of products, *no* imports were permitted if the Secretary determined that imports would (a) impair or reduce domestic production, or (b) interfere with the orderly domestic marketing or storing of the commodity, or (c) result in any unnecessary burden or expenditure under any government price support program. Imports of butter, nonfat dried milk solids, peanuts, peanut oil, flaxseed, linseed oil, and rice were prohibited and quantitative restrictions were placed on cheese.

The restrictions on the imports of cheese came at a rather unpropitious time, since the United States, under the Economic Cooperation Administration, had been encouraging certain countries, especially France, Italy and the Scandinavian countries, to expand production of cheese for the American market. Canada was also displeased, to put it lightly, at the reduction in access to the American market.

In mid-1953 Congress let Section 104 lapse, but it agreed to do so only after President Eisenhower had stated that he would impose essentially the same restrictions on imports of the affected fats and oils under the authority of Section 22, and other Administration spokesmen had promised that they would make Section 22 more "effective" than it had been in the past. Furthermore, Congress amended the Trade Agreements Act in mid-1953 so as to provide that the President, in an emergency, could impose Section 22 restrictions immediately; that is, without awaiting the recommendations of the Tariff Commission.

The relative arbitrariness of Section 104, together with the changes made in 1950 and 1951 which permitted Section 22 action to be taken regardless of the provision of any trade agreement or other international agreement, indicate the nature and significance of the schism between trade and agricultural policy. It is apparent that there is a strong tendency for many members of Congress, particularly those holding influential positions on the agricultural committees, to hold the position that no interference is to be allowed with any action affecting domestic agricultural interests or programs. International trade is a necessary evil, but an evil that must be controlled and restricted whenever possible.

Section 32 of Public Law 370, 75th Congress, authorized the Secretary of Agriculture to use up to 30 per cent of the gross customs receipts of the United States to expand domestic demand and to encourage the exportation of farm products. The latter provision obviously allowed export subsidies or export dumping.* While a large number of farm products have been subject to export subsidies at one time or another, the total export subsidies paid under Section 32 in 18 years has been only approximately $300 million, equal to about one-tenth of one per cent of the total value of exports of farm products during that period.

The most important export subsidy program, except for that now in operation for wheat, has been for cotton. This program was in operation before World War II and in the early post-war period. Before World War II, the subsidy rate was 1.5 cents a pound, or approximately 15 to 17 per cent of the market price. The export subsidy program was halted for a time during World War II, but was started again in 1944 and continued until 1948. The only other important export subsidy program has been the subsidies paid in connection with the International Wheat Agreement. From the start of the Agreement in 1949 through June 30, 1953, the total export subsidy was $558 million, and the cost for this fiscal year (1953-1954) will approximate $100 million. The subsidy cost under the Wheat Agreement is met by direct appropriation and is not paid from Section 32 funds.

* Export subsidies were also authorized by Section 12 of the Agricultural Adjustment Act of 1933.

It is also worth noting that last year the appropriation for the Mutual Security Act set aside $100 million to be used only to finance the export of agricultural products. The two main provisions in the enabling legislation were: (1) The U.S. Government would accept foreign currencies (at the official rates of exchange) in payment for the exports, with the aid dollars being used to purchase the commodities in the domestic market or from the Commodity Credit Corporation; (2) The exports under this provision were to be additional purchases by the importing country, purchases over and above what would otherwise be made.

IV. APPRAISAL OF THE FARM PROGRAMS

The United States price support and related programs can be appraised from several different viewpoints. We shall consider three—that of the United States consumer and taxpayer, that of the American farmer, and that of competing producers in other nations. Anticipating the conclusions—it would appear that at least until mid-1952 the American consumer and taxpayer fared reasonably well, the United States farmer may have gained relatively little, and foreign producers have on the whole been aided by the programs. These are rather different results than the supporters of the programs anticipated or than is commonly believed.

Let us first consider what the American consumer and taxpayer obtained for the $13 billion of tax funds spent on various farm programs related to the price support operations from mid-1933 through mid-1952. Approximately $9.4 billion of the total were in the form of direct payments to farmers, while the remainder was the losses on price support operations, domestic subsidies (school lunch program and food stamp plan, for example) and export subsidies. On the basis of fairly extreme assumptions about demand and assuming a zero elasticity of supply, total expenditure upon farm products over the period 1933-52 was increased by approximately $12 billion.* Thus the total cost to consumers and taxpayers might be set at a maximum of $25 billion.

* This estimate of the increase in consumer expenditures was derived as follows: The total loss on price support operations from 1933 through 1952 was approximately $3.6 billion, of which $600 million was the loss on potatoes and which is ignored in the calculation since the assumption of zero price elasticity of supply is clearly not valid. This leaves a net cost of $3 billion. The total gross receipts from farm production (excluding interfarm sales) was $328.4 billion. The estimate of cost to consumers was based on the assumption that the price support costs represented the cost of subsidizing sales of commodities, either in domestic or foreign markets. The price elasticity of demand in the "normal" market was assumed to be —0.25 and in the subsidized or low price market, —1.0. Thus total expenditure in the subsidized market remained unchanged, and the ratio of price support losses to gross receipts represented the propor-

But this is only a part of the story, and perhaps only a minor part. Contrary to original expectations, the overall effects of the farm programs, including price supports, were to increase farm output, and more importantly, to increase output per unit of input. Between 1925-29 and 1949-53, total farm output increased by 46 per cent and output per unit of input rose 39 per cent.†

There are several reasons for attributing at least part of the increase in technical efficiency (the rise in the ratio of output to input) to the farm programs. For one thing, where attempts were made to restrict the output of farm products by rationing land, farmers tried out methods of substituting other inputs for land and discovered that these methods of production were profitable even when the land input was not rationed. In addition, most of American agriculture was short on capital by the mid-thirties as a consequence of disinvestment during the first part of the decade. The rate of investment in agriculture was increased sharply in the late thirties, in part because of the large direct payments to farmers. Certain of the farm programs, particularly the soil conservation efforts, constituted a large scale extension or education program, with a feature that other educational activities lacked—namely, money to give to farmers. Finally, price supports by reducing uncertainty undoubtedly acted to induce farmers to try out new methods of production and to expend more on current inputs requiring cash expenditures.

If a fifth of the increase in the ratio of output to input were attributable to the farm price support and related programs and the same quantities of farm resources had been used during each of the years, the farm output forthcoming over the period in the absence of such programs would have been about 4 per cent less than it actually was. Assuming a price elasticity of demand of −0.25, total consumer expendi-

---

tionate reduction in supplies available in the "normal" market. This reduction amounted to 0.9 per cent and would imply an increase of 3.6 per cent in expenditures in the "normal" market or a total of about $12 billion.

Had the losses on potatoes been included and the same estimating procedure been followed, the total cost to consumers would have been $15 billion. However, the above estimate of $12 billion is definitely too high. Some consumers gained from the operations—the participants in the school lunch program and food stamp plan, for example. In addition, most of the losses by the Commodity Credit Corporation resulted from losses in sales from stocks in the general market, but at a later time than purchased. Such sales did not increase consumer expenditures during the period. The losses of the Commodity Credit Corporation on such sales amounted to about 40 per cent of the total price support costs.

† The construction of the indexes of output and input are described in United States Department of Agriculture, *Farm Production Practices, Costs and Returns*, Statistical Bulletin No. 83, Washington, D.C., October, 1949, pp. 7 and 74. However, the estimate of inputs used in the text differs from that published in the above reference since the price weights used here in the quantity index of inputs were averages for 1946-48 and the labor input was based on estimates made by the Bureau of Census.

tures would have been increased by about $36 billion for the last twenty years—far in excess of the direct tax expenditures and the estimated costs to consumers of export dumping and other price support costs. What this argument implies is that domestic expenditures on farm products might have been greater in the absence of the program than they have been with the program.*

The above line of argument also supports the conclusion that the income gains to farmers have been relatively small, if, indeed, any gains have accrued. This is a reasonable conclusion on other grounds as well. Given the structure of American agriculture, it is not an easy task to increase returns per unit of labor or per dollar invested in land or capital assets by tinkering with product prices. Since labor is continually leaving agriculture, an increase in the returns to labor (other things constant) will reduce the rate of outmovement of labor and thus increase agricultural output. The land market is sufficiently responsive to changes in expected returns that gains are rather quickly capitalized into the value of land. Thus, new entrants into farming gain little from an effective control over agricultural output, such as we have had in one instance—tobacco.

Competing foreign producers of agricultural products have been affected in various ways by our domestic farm programs. I am convinced that, if given a chance to cast a ballot, the foreign producers of cotton, tobacco, and sugar would vote to support the United States farm programs. The United States program has added considerable stability to world prices of cotton, and, while the hopes that American actions might result in higher prices for cotton may not have been realized, foreign cotton output has expanded materially during the period of our loan programs. Much of the basis for this expansion may have been the presumption that the United States would not allow cotton prices to again fall to the low levels of the early thirties.

Tobacco producers throughout the world have gained not only stability but probably higher prices. Tobacco is the one product in which output increases have been held in check somewhat and the United States has not resorted to export dumping to any important extent. Furthermore, tobacco prices have been stabilized around a moving upward trend.

The gains to foreign producers of sugar have arisen primarily because the existence of the sugar program has made possible a net reduction in the sugar tariff from 2 cents a pound to 0.5 cents a pound, though a part of this gain is offset by a processing or excise tax of 0.535 cents per pound, the proceeds being paid to domestic producers of sugar.

---

* A second possibility is that more resources would have been used in agriculture and that output in the rest of the economy would have been reduced as a consequence.

Despite the quotas on sugar imports, it would appear that the total value of sugar exports from Cuba to the United States is greater than it would be if there were no quota program and the higher tariff prevailed. If the tariff were 2 cents a pound instead of the present combined rate of 1.035 cents, Cuba would have to increase her shipments of sugar by almost 25 per cent in order to maintain the same dollar earnings, assuming the American retail sugar price remained at its present level. But if the import quotas were abandoned (unless Cuba instituted an export quota), the domestic price would probably fall since supplies available to the United States market would increase. Thus the monopolistic exploitation of American consumers is not without its benefits to the Cuban economy.

It is less clear what competing wheat producers would or should say about our wheat program. In 1949 and early 1950 and in 1953-1954 the loan program probably prevented a further sharp drop in world wheat prices. It is the reluctance of Congress to appropriate additional funds for export subsidies that is maintaining wheat at its present price in world markets, but it is also our present high support price that is preventing our wheat producers from reducing output. The latter consequence may well lead to lower world wheat prices in the future, if an attempt is made to liquidate our stocks.

Producers of dairy products in other countries have probably not been favorably impressed by our dairy support prices and the attendant restrictions on imports. It is doubtful, however, if much imported butter would be sold in the domestic market if we had no price supports on butter and only a nominal tariff. Cheese may be a different story, but even here imports were not very large before quotas were imposed.

Certain further comments may be made concerning the proposition that United States farmers have received little income gain from the farm price support and related programs of the past two decades. This conclusion is based upon two major considerations. First, and most important, the overall effect of the program has been to increase output per unit of input and thus to reduce the demand for farm resources. This is not intended to be a criticism of the program; in fact, the gains in technical efficiency have been of great significance to the American economy. Given the competitive character of agriculture and the low price elasticity of demand, the end result, except for tobacco, has been that farm products have been available to consumers at prices lower than what would have prevailed in the absence of the price support programs. But the effect on farm income is not that of increasing it.

Second, unless entry into agriculture is controlled, there is no reason to believe that returns to mobile resources would be increased by increasing the price of farm output. Any higher returns, in the short run,

will induce greater employment in agriculture and thus tend to drive down returns to the old level. Agriculture is particularly vulnerable to this kind of adjustment because there is a "normal" or usual outflow of labor from agriculture to nonagriculture. Labor employment can increase quickly through the process of slowing down the outflow. In addition, given the price policies of firms supplying such inputs to agriculture as machinery and fuel, the supply functions of many current inputs and short term investment items are almost perfectly elastic, at least in the short run. These and other influences mean that any income gains will be realized by the most immobile resource, namely land. If price supports are effective in increasing the value of farm marketings through time, it means that new entrants into agriculture will be faced with higher land prices and their net return on a dollar invested would be no greater than if the price support program had not been in effect. Thus, most of the gains go to the owners of land during the early years of the price support program. It is true, of course, that persons who inherit farm land do gain in the sense that the value of the asset would be greater than would otherwise have been the case. But it is doubtful if it is an appropriate objective of national policy to increase the incomes of those who inherit their land.

If price supports were effective in increasing farm incomes, what farmers would receive the major gains? In other words, would the income transfers be consistent with the generally accepted view that such transfers should be from the relatively rich to the relatively poor? We are here concerned with relatively short run effects, say from one to three or four years, before the resource adjustments described above have time to be completed.

A consideration of the income transfers involved in a price support program is pertinent because so much of the advocacy of farm price supports rests upon the view that farmers, on the average, represent a low income group. That the returns to farm labor is below returns to comparable labor in the rest of the economy can hardly be disputed. The large annual movement of farm people to nonfarm areas attests to this. But farm income is not all labor income, and contrary to general belief, nonlabor income is relatively more important for farm families than for nonfarm families. However, even after all the necessary adjustments for differences in purchasing power of income, the lower incidence of income taxes in agriculture, and for comparability of resources, the real returns to all farm families is probably below that of nonfarm families. But farm family income varies a great deal from one part of the country to another and the gains from farm price supports tend to be concentrated in the relatively high income groups in agriculture.

Let us at this point ignore the relatively low incomes in Southern agriculture and consider the group of farm families that would receive most of the gains from price supports. As is obvious, gains from price supports are closely related to the sales of farm products. Farm families that receive a large proportion of their income from the value of home produced food and housing or wages from nonfarm work are not much affected by the price supports. According to the 1950 Census of Agriculture, about 2.2 million farms (some 40 per cent of all farms) sold approximately 88 per cent of all farm products in 1949. The families of the operators of these farms had an average net annual income of $5,050. The average income of nonfarm families for the same year was about $5,100. However, the farm income represents a greater purchasing power than that of the nonfarm since almost 10 per cent of the farm income represents home produced food valued at farm sales prices. The same food purchased at retail would cost approximately twice as much, though the food would have some characteristics of value to farm families not available in the farm food. In terms of dollars of purchasing power equal to those of nonfarm families, the mean income of these 40 per cent of the farm families might approximate $5,500.

If we consider the incomes of the 1.23 million farm families that operate farms which sold 73 per cent of all farm products in 1949, we find that their net income was $6,350, or perhaps about $6,750 in dollars of nonfarm purchasing power. That is, the recipients of almost all of the gains from increased prices due to price supports would have been farm families with an average income above that of nonfarm families. But there is another relationship that is equally significant. The gains from higher prices would increase relative to income as farm family incomes increase, while the relative costs of higher food prices become more important as incomes of nonfarm families decrease. In other words, the largest gains go to the relatively well-to-do, while the greatest relative costs are paid by low income nonfarm families. This is not the way most citizens believe governmental authority should be used to transfer income from one group to another.

Up to this point, our general appraisal of farm price support programs has been in terms of the operations until mid-1952. At that time the price supports had not significantly overvalued farm products, at least when viewed *ex post*, except in the case of wheat and certain fats and oils. The stocks of most farm products, either in government or private hands, were relatively low and barely exceeded normal working stocks. Wheat stocks were at low levels because of the large export subsidies, but corn, cotton, and tobacco had been moving quite freely into normal trade channels. But during 1952-1953 and 1953-1954, the demand-supply situation for most farm products changed quite drastically. Farm prices started their post-Korean decline in February, 1951 and the

parity ratio declined from 113 in that month to 94 in January, 1953, reached a low of 90 in December, 1953 and was 94 in January, 1954. The decline in relative farm prices cannot be attributed to the slowing down of demand growth for the economy as a whole, which apparently did not start until mid-1953. The downward movement of farm prices had been completed, in large part, six months prior to that time.

It would appear that nothing short of a war or a strong inflationary movement could significantly increase the parity ratio over the next few years. The export demand for several important farm products has declined substantially since 1948 as output in other parts of the world has recovered from the early postwar lows. Foreign production of cotton in 1952 was 50 per cent above 1948, while the output of wheat, rice, tobacco, and fats and oils also has expanded significantly. The post World War II adjustment of farm prices to peace conditions was interrupted by the Korean conflict, and the high farm prices of late 1950 and early 1951 were due primarily to attempts to increase inventories, especially in Europe, rather than to any basic changes in supply conditions and consumer demand.

Because of the characteristics of the demand and supply functions for farm products, particularly their low price elasticities, it is hazardous to make predictions as to the general level of farm prices over a period of time as long as five years. If total production, because of unusually favorable weather or more rapid technical change than expected, should increase by three per cent more than anticipated, relative farm prices might be 6 to 12 per cent lower than predicted. The contrary could also occur—if output failed to increase as rapidly as expected, relative farm prices might increase to the same degree compared to the level predicted. Similarly, shifts in demand due to changing tastes, population growth, or inflation can have comparable effects. The influence of inflation or deflation is worthy of mention because of the stickiness of certain cost elements in the marketing structure.

By the summer and fall of 1954 carryover of wheat will equal 800 million bushels (70 to 90 per cent of annual production); corn, 750 million bushels (22 to 26 per cent of a crop); cotton, 9.5 million bales (60 to 75 per cent of output); and fats and oils, 1,700 million pounds (30 per cent of domestic disappearance). There is no reasonable expectation that control measures in effect in 1954 will result in a reduction in these stocks by mid-1955, or in 1956 for that matter. It is most unlikely that acreage restrictions on corn, cotton and wheat will have any significant effect on the output of these products. No one—farmers or their political representatives—wants the acreage reductions to be large enough to have an appreciable impact on production. The present legislation called for a reduction in upland cotton acreage to 17.9 million acres in 1954; however, Congress recently enacted special legislation increasing acreage allotments by 3.5 million acres. The net reduction from acreage from the 1953 level will be about 4 million acres. This small reduction in acreage can be offset in large part by additional use of fertilizer and more intensive cultural practices. And, of course, every farmer will remove the least well adapted land from cotton.

The acreage limitation on wheat is more severe (from 79 million acres seeded in 1953 to 62 million acres for 1954). Some output reduction will occur in 1954, though it will be limited by the selection of land retained in wheat by each farmer and the application of more intensive practices in the more humid areas. In 1955 and subsequent years, the effect of the acreage reduction will be relatively limited in the Great Plains States because of the effect of increased summer fallow. The corn acreage reduction will be relatively small since the only sanction against non-compliance is the inability of the farmer to obtain a non-recourse loan. But most corn farmers feed all the corn they produce and so this sanction is relatively unimportant. And even if corn acreage were reduced, the land would be used to produce other feeds that are ready substitutes for corn.

American agriculture has a high degree of flexibility. It was this flexibility that permitted large increases in output during World War II. But it was this same flexibility that largely negated the efforts to restrict farm output in the late thirties and early forties and will probably defeat the same methods when tried in the future.

There is therefore little likelihood that acreage limitations will be capable of reducing or even stabilizing stocks of farm commodities. Unless the United States embarks upon extensive export dumping devices, the present price support program may fall from its own weight. Since there is no real evidence that the program has effectively increased farm income, or is capable of doing so in the future, the next year or so represents a time in which a reconsideration of farm price supports may be most appropriate.

V. A SUGGESTED FARM PRICE POLICY

The proposals which President Eisenhower made to Congress in January, 1954, included two major features. The first was that the basic provisions of the Agricultural Act of 1949 be allowed to become effective: the variable price schedules in January, 1955, and the modernized parity the following year. The second was the proposal to "insulate" from the market a large part of the existing government-held surpluses by creating an emergency reserve, together with a provision that might make it possible to use the variable price schedule for the basic crops and

18

to rely less upon the use of acreage allotments and marketing quotas. The President's proposals are certainly a step in the right direction in reducing the area of conflict between trade and agricultural policy and in eventually reducing price support levels from their present unrealistic levels.

But the task of reconciling agriculture and trade policies requires a sharper break with past price policies than is involved in the President's proposals. An obvious way out would be to discontinue all price supports. But this is not only unlikely for sheer political reasons; it also might not represent the optimum policy for the United States. A strong case can be made, however, for a policy of forward prices that would aid farmers in making their production plans, reduce risk and uncertainty confronting farmers, and provide some protection against the incidence of depression. In essence, a forward price policy involves estimates of the market prices that would equilibrate supply and demand. These estimates would be made by a governmental agency and announced in advance of the time important production decisions have to be made. In order to reduce and transfer uncertainty, the government would guarantee price returns equal to some major fraction, say 90 per cent, of the estimated price.*

During periods of full employment such a price policy would not be designed to influence the level of farm prices. The objective would be to present farmers with as accurate forecasts as possible of anticipated prices prior to the time most production decisions are made. Except when the estimates of anticipated prices were in error, no price supporting operations would occur. However, there are some circumstances in which the price estimates will be in error, namely for products whose output cannot be predicted with a fair degree of accuracy. This includes most of the farm crops since their actual yield does not depend entirely upon the inputs controlled by man. Because of the low price elasticity of demand for most farm crops, a large yield usually results in a substantial reduction in the gross income from the crop.

There are two main ways of handling the price variability that would result from yield variations. For the storable crops (corn, wheat, cotton, tobacco, rice and many feed grains) the government could adopt a storage program that would reduce market offerings from large crops and increase market supplies when crops are small. If the objective of the storage policy were to stabilize use of the products rather than to stabilize prices, the storage program would not be inconsistent with relatively free trade in the major exported and imported farm products.

* For details, see my *Forward Prices for Agriculture* (Chicago, 1947) and *Trade and Agriculture, A Study of Inconsistent Policies* (New York, 1950), especially pp. 92-125.

For the crops which cannot be stored except at high cost, the forward prices should be not a single price, but a schedule of prices that would approximately stabilize total revenue. The forward price would be an estimate of prices if yield were average; the schedule would translate the expected total revenue from an average crop into a series of prices for relevant yields.

In addition to the two techniques described above, it would be essential that the method used to guarantee the farmers the forward price when expectations were in error not interfere with the flow of the commodity into domestic and international trade. Major reliance should be placed upon direct payments to producers if the forward price were higher than actual market price. Thus markets would be allowed to clear, except as it was desirable to add to stocks from a relatively large output of a storable crop.

During a depression, if one should occur, it would be advisable to establish forward prices at a level above that which would be an estimate of market prices. This procedure would have several advantages. First, it would mean that the treatment of agricultural producers would be roughly comparable to the treatment of other groups in the economy. Second, the policy would constitute an additional means of preventing the cumulative destruction of purchasing power that normally occurs during the downturn of the cycle. There can be no doubt that price support operations during 1949 and again during late 1953 were of value in maintaining money income in the economy and in preventing a greater decline in economic activity. Third, the maintenance of a relatively high level of income in agriculture would serve to maintain employment in certain rather volatile sectors of the economy, particularly in farm machinery.

The means for meeting the price commitments should be the same as during a full employment period. Storage programs should be continued to partially offset output variations, though no attempt should be made to offset the decline in demand by increasing stocks during the depression. The techniques used in establishing the forward price levels during a depression would probably have to be somewhat arbitrary. Certain guidelines might be established, however. Relative farm product prices should not depart far from the relationship in the immediately preceding full employment period, and, further, the absolute level of forward prices should reflect a downward drift in prices paid by farmers. Further, it would be reasonable to permit some decline in real farm income in order that farmers not be given a preferred income position during the depression. However, the decline in real income should be fairly moderate— perhaps 15 to 20 per cent—if the program is to have the advantages referred to above. It should be added that the proposal for forward

prices during a depression is not intended as a substitute for an integrated monetary and fiscal policy for the stabilization of employment at high levels. It is suggested as one element in a broad-gauged attack upon the prevention of a cumulative downswing and would be relatively impotent in a serious downswing if concerted activity were not used in other directions.

The price proposals suggested here are not intended to result in an income transfer to farm people during full employment periods. It was argued earlier that such income transfers are not likely to have any significant long run effect upon the return to labor engaged in agriculture. In addition, the short run transfers tend to go primarily to the highest income groups in agriculture. The proposal is made in the present form, not because it is argued that there is no problem of low incomes in agriculture, but rather that price policy is an ineffective means of contribution to the solution of such problems.

There are a large number of farm families, perhaps a million or more, who now realize less from the employment of their labor in agriculture than could be obtained if the same labor were employed elsewhere. There has been and continues to be a large transfer of labor force from agricultural to nonagricultural employments. But this transfer has not been rapid enough to bring real returns to comparable labor in agricultural and nonagricultural pursuits into approximate equality. During the past decade large changes have occurred in agriculture on this score. In the late thirties it was true for almost the whole of the United States that the returns to farm labor were substantially below the returns to comparable and employed nonfarm labor. Admittedly the high level of unemployment that prevailed in the nonfarm sector as late as early 1941 makes comparisons of this sort questionable, but it is worthy of note that by the end of World War II most of the differences in labor returns had disappeared, except for the southern states, most of Missouri, and an area immediately north of the Ohio River. Transfer of labor out of agriculture in the non-southern areas has continued, and the income differential sufficient to induce the movement is a relatively small one. However, in the south (and the other areas noted), the income differential that is associated with the current rate of outmovement is a very large one, of the order of $500 to $1,000 a year of labor.

There is little evidence that farm price policy has contributed or can contribute anything to narrowing this difference. It seems reasonable to argue that more information and more accurate information about alternative employment opportunities would help to increase the rate of labor transfer. Direct assistance to movement, such as locating jobs prior to movement, loans or grants to pay the cost of moving and to cover living expenses prior to the first pay check, and assistance in locating housing might have a substantial impact. In the longer run, improving the quality of primary and secondary education in the low income agricultural areas might have the most substantial impact of all.

VI. THE PROBLEMS OF TRANSITION

There have been times in the past when it would not have been at all difficult to change from the then current price support programs to one such as that outlined above, assuming agreement as to the desirability of the change. But such is not the case today. The large stocks of many farm commodities that exist at present, or will exist in the near future, constitute a real barrier to any modification of farm price programs. If these stocks were abruptly released and placed upon the market, price declines of 25 to 50 per cent could be expected in many instances. It would take from one to two years before current demand for consumption and production once again became the dominant price determining considerations.

So drastic a readjustment in prices would mean the political doom of any new price program. This was recognized by President Eisenhower in his proposal to establish a special emergency reserve of farm products. This reserve would be sterilized and withdrawals would be made only under special conditions, such as in case of war or to meet emergency situations arising in friendly nations. While the justification for establishing a stockpile of farm products on the grounds of military necessity rests on somewhat dubious grounds if we were starting from scratch, so to speak, there may be some merit in trying to create some virtue out of past and present vices. The large stocks of farm products which existed in 1941 and again in 1950 reduced somewhat the difficulties of the transition to a war economy. And it might be argued that if we were to be subjected to aerial attack in another war, the value of appropriately dispersed food reserves might be substantial. But, in trying to make virtue out of vice, we should not forget the costs of such a program. Ignoring the costs of the commodities themselves (and thus the interest upon their value), it would cost between 15 and 20 cents per year per bushel to store wheat and corn, for example. Thus, to store for a decade a billion bushels, which are readily available, would cost between $1.5 billion and $2 billion. This is a large total cost in some absolute sense, but some perspective may be gained by comparing it with one's estimate of total defense expenditures for the same span of time.

However, some of the commodities for which there are large stocks, such as butter and cottonseed oil, may not be so readily or easily maintained as defense reserves. Certainly there is no reasonable ground for maintaining stocks of butter, with the original high input cost and

22

relatively rapid deterioration in storage, when much cheaper substitutes exist. In those instances in which there is inadequate justification for inclusion of a commodity in a defense reserve, a policy should be followed of placing only a certain proportion of existing governmentally owned or controlled stocks upon the market during a specified time period. During the time of liquidation, a support price should be established for the product, but this should not be a price maintained in the market. The market price should be allowed to go free and the producers should then be paid the difference between the support price and the market price. During this transition period some effort should be made to establish the support price at a level which would equate the amount produced and the amount consumed if the stock liquidation were not occurring.

As has been noted before, the present farm price support situation is untenable. Despite the strong appeal which many politicians believe high support prices have, it is unlikely that the present price support program can be maintained much longer. It is true that the transition to a price support or forward price policy that can be operated successfully over a period of time will be relatively painful to both farmers and the taxpayers, though presumably not to consumers. But such a transition seems to be in the offing.

VII. CONCLUSION*

During the past two decades, our efforts to achieve greater liberalization of international trade frequently have been accommodated to the actual or presumed needs of our agricultural price support programs.

* It has not been possible in a short essay to discuss all the issues relevant to the interrelations and inconsistencies between international trade and agricultural policy. Two important omissions may be noted—problems arising from price instability in internationally traded products, and the implications of our efforts to aid certain areas of the world in their economic development. The omission of the second—aid to economic development in low income countries—may be justified on the ground that the changes in comparative advantage that may result cannot be predicted at this time. In any case, such changes as may occur in the demand for American farm products—either in a favorable or unfavorable direction—will be spread over a sufficient period of time to permit gradual adjustments.

The first omission is more serious, however, and can be justified, if at all, only on the grounds that we know so little about the possibility of reducing the erratic, short run instability of prices of many internationally traded goods. Reference may be made to the price behavior of wool and jute during 1950, 1951, and 1952. Wool prices increased more than 150 per cent between the first half of 1950 and the first quarter of 1951 and then declined by 60 per cent by the third quarter of 1951. Jute prices increased by more than 150 per cent between the second half of 1950 and the second quarter of 1951 and then declined by 75 per cent by the third quarter of 1952. These violent changes resulted primarily from variations in the willingness to hold inventories, and, in the case of jute, from the response of producers to the very high price in mid-1951.

It may be noted that the proposals outlined in Section V would go some distance in

While the trade restrictions and export subsidization have had the effect of protecting and expanding American farm output and thus creating some inefficiency in the use of our resources, perhaps the most important consequence has been the picture of American indecision and inconsistency that we have created in the minds of our friends and allies. Our vacillation between freeing and restricting trade has certainly cast doubts upon both our sincerity and our ability to carry forward constructive international economic policies.

Most of the adjustments that are required for consistency in our trade and agricultural policies require modification of the farm price policies. The current price policies require various forms of interferences with trade in order that specific price programs can operate without the accumulation of exceptionally large stocks or requiring large expenditures from the Treasury. However, at the present time even with the absolute prohibition of some imports (butter, for example) and large export subsidies on others (wheat), stocks of many farm commodities have become so large as to create significant problems of management.

The required modification of the farm price policies would not be damaging to the income position of labor employed in agriculture for the past and present farm programs have not had any significant influence on labor incomes in agriculture. In most of American agriculture the level of labor incomes is dependent primarily upon the availability of jobs in the nonfarm sector and upon the relative ease of changing from farm to nonfarm jobs, not upon the level of farm price supports.

---

minimizing the effects of this type of price variability upon the plans made by farmers and upon their incomes. The forward prices would serve as guides for production planning and the guarantees implicit in the proposals would at least moderate the effects on income of drastic downturns in prices that occur at times.